DE'LURE
PUBLISHING

MENTAL APEX

DE'LURE PUBLICATIONS PRESENTS

MENTAL APEX

INVISIBLE PYRAMIDS

DE'LURE

De'Lure Publishing

De'Lure

The author has represented and warranted full ownership and/or legal right to publish all the materials in this book.

"MENTAL APEX"

Invisible Pyramids

De'Lure

Never let anyone actively steal your JOY, your SANITY, your IMAGINATION, or your DREAMS. My art is for everyone who wants to experience it, but if you know PERSONALLY how it feels to be unjustly attacked or ridiculed on extraordinary levels my words are even more so for you. Do me a favor and ENJOY the SANITY of your DREAMS. In the end MEDIOCRITY cannot COEXIST in the midst of AMAZING! IN HUMBLE EXCELLENCE WE WILL REIGN SUPREME... Welcome to APEX

"*APEX*"

(7-23-16)

Aptly accepting ascension into my Mental Apex...

Mentally manifesting more power

as I mold my own Matrix...

The safest surest bet

to malign and mutilate all self-Mediocrity...

Putting the PROPER predicates forth

to POWER my own Philosophy...

I adopted me properly,

I had to REBIRTH my conscious and True Origin...

I couldn't continue to EVOLVE a mind

drowned in premeditated Moral Sin...

I choose to WIN... failure is a disease

and my brain has become the Ultimate Cure...

I put pen to pad, they TASTED my thoughts,

and was born a talent Pure...

Obscure, and Outlandish,

but never Obtuse or Obligatory...

There is no norm, or a thing set in stone,

nothing at all is Mandatory...

We move and cultivate

*as we Create, **Corral**, and Conquer...*

De'Lure

patiently prodding a people in PAIN

as I paint my poems and Prosper...

Could have been a doctor

or a career educator like my MOM...

But the passion that captured my heart

was manufacturing literary BOMBS...

Intertwining Words, Ideas, and Fictional Lives

Is more than LIFE to Me...

Whole worlds at my fingertips

as soulful emotions BLEED, inside of me...

My thoughts breed in spite of me

I even write books in my DREAMS...

Sometimes a new-found POWER and PREMISE

is EVERYTHING He Seems...

APEX, all the invisible pyramids are here

if only you'd OPEN your eye...

3 of a kind, your 3rd eye blind, as I ESCAPE in the

clouds I FLY...

"*Alive*"

(4-20-17)

De'Lure

How could I fall down

a thousand more times

When all but the pyramids

were blinded by the lies of false crimes

Never cry, hide, or confide in those guys

Instead fly high while widening stranger's eyes

To your inevitable prize

It's never enough to be wise

If you don't utilize your gifts to guide

I find myself alive

With eyes only the Heavens could provide

When they throw stones at my glass shoes

I improvise

Foundation is everything

And in all things, find your drive to thrive

Unbreakable, but I was shakable

I felt your venom but I ate it

The masses want success

But with ease I bait it, create it, and slay it

What God has for me is PATIENT, WAITING, and

AMAZING

Racing, dancing on my hands

Across scorching sands ablazing

Outdated but still before my time

Procrastination and over calculation

Were my only true crimes

The sun gave me my lines

While the moon and stars

Consistently urge me to shine

I run full speed to the center of the sanctuary

From there I climb

How dare they try to bastardize and patronize

My quiet rise

STILL...

I... Am... Alive!!!

"*Where were you...*"

(7-20-12)

Underneath the umbrella tree...

I was left alone and naked

for the world to see...

Confused and alone

placating my own emotional wounds...

I was a fool to think

that her love was real and true...

The animals were loose

and left to his and her own devices...

So, I ran away in my own mind

pretending it didn't happen had to suffice...

Suffice it to say,

my young mind could never run far enough away...

So again, I'd wait

and then placate, medicate, and meditate...

I hope she never had a clue

what they were choosing to do...

But my mind was so thorough as a child

I had already broken through...

To the truth, through the pain

that ran cold in my veins...

De'Lure

Like harsh methodic black rain...

unstoppable like a devilish runaway train...

No one can be that blind

to what transpires in their own domain...

I in my own mind knew, she knew

and cast out any living doubt...

I was angry left without options

no wonder I began lashing out!!!...

I couldn't even reach the light switch

I was too small for the nightmares...

And just because so many other children know my pain

doesn't make it fair...

You take away the innocence of a brilliant child

you then plant an extraordinary seed...

He can't see the good your bad is doing at the time

as his mind and body begin to bleed...

He has no choice but to cry and concede...

In the quiet time

his brain cells begin to breathe, feed, seethe...

But after he escapes the demons

and becomes then a man...

If he survives he'll evolve

and unleash a breathtaking plan...

I understand that my audience

AT TIMES can't understand my mind...

I also understand that I was created

to write, evoke emotions, and then shine...

I never wanted the spotlight

but it comes along with the rise of rare talent...

So, I keep my demons at bay

for now, focus on my future and stabilize the balance...

Be not surprised, as I shine,

and the product of my mind is fully revealed...

The moment I was broken as a child

my genius fate was forever sealed...

"Love Costs"

(3-11-17)

Mental Apex

She's so close to perfection
it always pains me to see her fall short
I'm dying just to baby her,
but she's never been the pampering sort
She only needs me when I'm not around,
my love is her last resort
Sarcastic retorts, masked emotions, all tucked away
inside red lace bras and boy shorts
Her body is exquisite, but it was her lips and eyes
that forced me to come undone
How can I be the man for a woman
who's convinced she doesn't even need one
All I can do is let the truth live
as my emotions continue to run
Loving her is akin to a twisted rollercoaster
whose peaks and valleys are never done
But that's not my gripe
I don't need her to be one of those breakable trophy wives
I'm psyched that her mind shines
and moves at the speed of light
Her eyes they shutter and fly
through the blissful skies of my mind
like vibrant yellow butterflies
I just want to forever be the knight in adequate armor
to kiss her when she shuts her eyes
Taken aback by the fact
that she's giving our future the possibility of doom
But believing she's not changing as she's aging
is far too much to assume
The second most common reason for divorce in the U.S.
so to speak is falling asleep in the bedroom
But conscious burning desires don't have to be relit
and sometimes all a man needs is some headroom
Let's assume the gloom
that may loom is not her fault

14

De'Lure

But that now she has simply become
from my past actions, what she was taught
Maybe I was more accessible
to the masses than I ought
But precious pennies and premeditated passion
is what I've consistently spent on her thoughts
Love Costs

"A Woman Distraught"

(7-21-16)

De'Lure

Stuck in between single
and a hard place...
sometimes I look in the mirror
and wonder do I have a hard face...
My brain is more
than just a smart space...
I have hopes and dreams
I want something I can claim...
Being this alone all the time
is just a damn shame...
Even when I have a man here
I often don't know the right thing to say...
It never really matters
cause in my heart they're all just playing games...
I mean in the first place
I have a good heart
and nice shape...
I'm the type of girl
that can cook, clean, and sex my man late...
Late at night
when I should probably be asleep...
I'd climb on top of Love
and help him guide inside me deep...
But does this matter
or any of my thoughts...
What about my ass
and all this expensive lingerie I've bought...
Should I be a good girl
or just a real freak...
I mean I want a good man
but he's gotta be one I can keep...
All the words I'm speaking are true
even though I couldn't put em together myself...
So inboxed my homie De'Lure
he swore that he could help...

He said I could go inside your mind
and pull new poetry out...
I'm sitting there like dude you cool or whatever
but that I seriously doubt...
We started talking he started writing
I still thought that he was lying...
now I'm just like you reading this poem
and girl now I'm just complying...
that boy is good
his mind is something to behold...
I read "Take My Breath Away" Orlando Nights
and then every story he's ever told...
He told me my soulmate is searching for me
just as hard as I'm searching for him...
I took him at his word and when Mr. Right is ready
I'll be right here waiting for him...

"Invisible Princesses"

(1-20-17)

Mental Apex

They're all dying inside

and it's many of our faults...

The damage we created and caused

could have been avoided if we had been taught...

In turn our misery is what we bought...

Don't you dare tell a lady to act like a woman

if you weren't there to teach her how...

When so many of us are absentee fathers

how can we possibly look down or frown...

Every girl still owns her crown...

If she grew up with her King and Queen together

the luster in her crown should still remain...

But if she grew up with one or neither

her nonexistent shine is probably occupied by eternal pain...

She can't stand the rain...

Every little girl needs her daddy

whether it be biological or otherwise...

A potent paternal figure

who can placate fears and preclude lies...

Dry her tear stained eyes...

At times, We are the reason

some women have become undateable...

The ones that never knew what love from a man was,

to that concept they're unrelatable...

These distractions are unfadable...

Now, It's not always our fault

sometimes a little girl's mother stands in the way...

Once or twice every week

should be daddy-daughter day...

This is the only way...

If you procreate you need to Communicate, Appreciate,

and Reciprocate real love...

But if you never knew what that love felt like, it becomes easy to medicate

and hide behind alcohol and drugs...

Tuning out the world with your earbuds...

I propose a new world and a new day

there's nothing else we can do...

If you don't want to be a father

be careful who and how you screw...

Sometimes after the hammer hits the nail

you'll wish the balls were blue...

That fact rings true, as men we can pick up the pieces

of any woman's crown...

Or we can continue to objectify her

as her heart, soul, and mind openly drown...

Her dignity is in the lost and found...

I taught MYSELF to never complain

if I didn't have a solution to a problem...

So, in retrospect I sit alone silently

thinking about things until I solve them...

My mind is ever evolving...

If each person can find stability first and then a mate

in which they're equally yoked...

Then together we can ALL begin to view the world

and our lives through a vibrant rainbow-colored scope...

YOU and I, WE and Us, are each other's

ONLY HOPE

"*Broken Rainbows*"

(1-31-17)

Broken rainbows and butterscotch nightmares...

Dark chocolate raindrops

dripping down cracked coconut stairs...

Watermelon whispers wafting through the darkness

never knowing where their journey will end...

Licorice lies crafted by bitter jealousies

no truth could ever mend...

Pumpkin spice promises

promoted with pretentious power...

Soaked with green apple spit

and the spite to spin a soul sour...

We are all alone

even when we feel the most surrounded...

Love is a passive, divisive, entity

born to confound us...

I used to write that we all need love

but that's just simply not true...

I need look no further than my own vomit stained mirror

to find real significant proof...

They judge you and they judge me

our plights are much the same...

De'Lure

I won't place blame or take aim

I'll just slowly lobby for change...

Yes, life is a game and most days

I no longer want to play...

Smiles they come and go

they were never meant to stay...

They assault my face in random ways

then quickly pass away...

All life, if it lasts,

eventually fades to gray...

Like the birth of a baby boy

opposed to twenty years after your wedding day...

Everything seems perfect in the beginning

then reality sets in...

They say aging and changing are blessings

what about when two decades of vows abruptly end...

I've never been married

so, I don't pretend to know that pain...

But being the product of a broken home

I do understand the chain...

Maybe I'm here for a purpose

far deeper than my mama ever thought...

Maybe my battle is deeper

than every demon I've ever fought...

Words are my Band-Aids

and poetry is my shield from life...

But if ever they escape me, kindly erase me,

with blissful bullets and cold knives...

"Cherry's Bloom"

(6-18-16)

And so I asked myself

do Cherry's bloom...

And since her eyes shine bright like the moon

I knew full well LOVE would soon loom...

See George Washington

never really chopped down that cherry tree...

But the angels

really sent down Cherry for me...

Her eyes, nose, and mouth

All hypnotic to my soul...

Capturing her heart

would be the greatest love story ever told...

I imagine waking up every day

knowing you'll always be there...

Smiling as I open my eyes

tickled by your soft curly hair...

Holding you ever so tightly

your slender body pressed hard against mine...

I Need to know you better though

and the only gift I'd accept from you is time...

De'Lure

Your hand in marriage would be a plus too

but we're both still young...

But then how can I fawn for wedding bells

when yesterday was the first time I tasted your sweet tongue...

I could stare at you forever,

but does that make me special? Hell no...

With a face that proves God is real

anyone could get lost in your sweet glow...

I'm a hopeless romantic

full of real hope when I'm around you...

Honestly no man can even breathe in your airspace

I'm no exception I drown too...

"Bleed Me"

(12-7-16)

The cars SWAY from lane to lane...

The bullets they SPRAY...

Extracting blood and brains

from everybody they entered and CHANGED...

All left on HORRIFIC display

for those of us who REMAIN...

Sustained or so stained...

I got HIT too

I just HEAL a little bit quicker...

Blood trickles as I'm GUIDED and prided

by the LIGHT in my mind that eternally flickers...

The constant DRAIN depression becomes

the ONLY mainstay...

Even viewing LIFE through rose colored glasses

they mostly SEE their days

in fifty shades of GRAY...

We PRAY day after day for change

but we too are DERANGED...

Because the CHANGE for which in large part we pray

involves how much CASH we can obtain...

Being Materialistic is a mind state;

one as a PEOPLE we facilitate, incubate, and appreciate...

Never close your eyes

we are LIVING in the Sponge Bob age...

Trump is our president maybe now you BELIEVE

when they say, we are living in the LAST DAYS...

Sweet America the home of the FREE... Or is it...

When MOST American children and adults

sit online all day and just FIDGET...

Slaves to our phones, slaves to our homes,

our existences just DRONE on and on...

Never on a soapbox but I'm up out of my BUBBLE

and back in my comfort zone...

I tell them all never complain

unless you have a forming SOLUTION...

Never CONFORMING to negative musings

you must pay attention to how you do things...

You have to TEACH them

but they do not have to learn or ever be PERFECT...

Wisdom has to be yearned, earned, and then burned

into the brain's SURFACE...

Illumination is not for the faint at heart,

learn to SURRENDER

De'Lure

without also falling apart...

Destroy perceived, permanent, public perceptions

without tipping over the APPLECART...

I too cannot complain

without a solution for this Age...

I could just continue to BUILD myself

without ever REACHING OUT to turn the world's page...

Unlike the status quo

I feen for real LASTING change...

I no longer CARE who and how they ruin my face

I'm in a GOOD space...

When I look in the mirror I SEE humbly

what I LOVE and CREATE...

Admitting now all of my PAST has largely had a strange fate,

but we live on to FIGHT another day...

Tragic and traumatic

are the names of my HISTORY until this moment...

I was TORMENTED on higher levels than most

because I was CHOSEN...

The BULLETS they shot were piercing and painful

but I myself was never permanently BROKEN...

The FUTURE is potent, De'Lure

Hone in...

"Blind Ears"

(1-17-17)

De'Lure

Rewind time set aside those that remain BLIND

as we try to CLIMB...

As we try to find higher PLATFORMS of illumination

in which WE can reside...

In time our worlds will inevitably COLLIDE

and we will be FORCED to awaken or kill the blind...

Time is very REAL and too precious

to be wasted on DEAF cries...

Mute out all the LIES and white noise

from the bleachers...

We are all broken but MENDABLE creatures...

The enlightened should be TEACHERS

but we're mostly just all DEAD or features...

On some egregious, facetious, NEWS article

designed for incredibly IGNORANT readers...

It's impossible to know TRUTH from a lie

when the LIE is what you prefer...

And it's IMPOSSIBLE to be illuminated

when the DARK is what you serve...

But these things OCCUR

and IDIOTS will not be deterred or differed...

Affirmative action is more than just a verb

and it must be EMBEDDED and functionally learned...

Black lives matter but we ENJOY nothing more

than the RIPPING down of a gracefully ascending black man...

He doesn't have to BOTHER a soul

nope no one really gives a DAMN...

He's POSITIVE and TALENTED

we need him to FALL now!!!

His light is shining too BRIGHT

there's absolutely NO WAY to put it out...

As he begins to FLY

his wings are causing the evil echoes to DROWN and fade out...

Lesson learned, FEELINGS no longer hurt,

as HE turns and waves to the crowd...

Mama is PROUD

"*Cheating Death*"

(1-25-17)

My shadows and I followed IDLY

by a parade of HUNGRY black cats...

Trouncing triumphantly over BROKEN mirrors

and sidewalk CRACKS...

Clothed in POPULAR sneakers and comfortable hoodies

we never wanted them to FEAR US...

But burdened and blessed with the VOICE of the colored children

we just wanted them to HEAR US...

Tear me down no more my PROGRESS is for

every black child who was ever told NO...

I EXCEED expectations and spawn transcendence

because my MIND says so...

If we CHOOSE to grow slow

at a point, we'll be LEFT BEHIND to die...

Choose instead to blaze your own PATH

and so THRIVE...

I transcribe stories from PURE imagination

because that's what keeps MY SANITY flowing...

Life is like riding a bike to keep your BALANCE

you have to KEEP GOING...

This was Einstein's take

who am I to challenge his GENIUS...

And when they said ALL men are created equal

De'Lure

how come they DIDN'T MEAN US...

Not meant to BLINSIDE you

but welcome to the FEELING of being a black man in America...

Where any little slip up, the wrong outfit, or a SLEIGHT of tongue

can END OUR LIVES and cause HYSTERIA...

They MARCH after the blood is already spilled

they CRY for wounds that can NEVER BE HEALED...

What about the LIVING

don't we deserve to be LOVED and REVERED...

Being ROBBED of my POWER or the RELEVANCE of my voice

has ALWAYS been my BIGGEST fear...

Shedding NO MORE tears

we DROWN old SORROWS with stale beers...

The LACK of SUPPORT and OPPORTUNITY for my brothers

in Corporate America is CRSYTAL CLEAR...

So what, I'm HERE, the FUTURE needs my words

more than I need HER...

So, I'll keep POUNDING the PULSING production pavement

UNTIL they call me SIR!!!

"*Dry Tears*"

(Christmas Day 2016)

I don't even know how to CRY anymore...

I see the INFECTED wounds

but I can't even tell if they're still SORE...

Blood curdling SCREAMS

cry out from my CORE...

I'm trying to UNDERSTAND the beat

but my heart and mind are still TORN...

Forlorn looks on my SICK face

are commonplace now...

I SEE and FEEL chapped lips,

heavy feet, and downtrodden brows...

When people tell me I'm ATTRACTIVE now,

I drown out the sound...

It's all white noise

I can NEVER see what they've found...

I see what I see

when I see me an AGING BLACK CLOWN...

Life is a sarcastic JOKE

choking away ANY good memories...

And caring about how you look

apparently TRANSLATES into homosexual tendencies...

I'm OFFENSIVE you see

even when I'm just DYING in my OWN skin...

My momentary pseudo HAPPINESS

causes the onlookers much CHAGRIN...

My back was created to BEND,

my body to be BEATEN in every imaginable way...

My pores are SICK and WIDE with invitation

my sweat DRIPS like POISON rain...

My old knees yet to BUCKLE

continue to PAINFULLY rock and sway...

Like the wind that blows through the mossy trees

on another MEANINGLESS Southern day...

My thoughts are FLEETING

it's hard now to understand my own mind...

Unwind the twine in my cerebellum

and only CONFUSION you'll find...

I'm still FUNCTIONAL I suppose,

I go through daily motions by DESIGN...

But I long for the days END

when I can DROWN in my rough hotel pillows and CRY...

Yet dying is the SWEETEST thought

I'll ever fathom or know...

Death will show them all

long after there's no mud left to throw...

Attacking a once BEAUTIFUL MIND

ends well for no one it simply DISRUPTS the flow...

Seventy times seven days in a DESTRUCTIVE mind state

where else can the genius go...

All alone where he belongs

he was constructed to be OUTCAST...

Bullets, knives, and insults whistle well

as they flee INSIDE me and past...

He makes them all believe he's UNREACHABLE

to their NEVER-ENDING grasps...

But deep in his own SUBCONCIOUS he has already lost

and all he can do is gasp...

Hate Don't Last Always... But Love Don't Either.

"A Lover's Portion..."

(Valentine's Day 2016)

De'Lure

Every time the wind blows
her hair is the only SCENT I smell...
After the others CAME and LEFT
for her love is the ONLY one I fell...
Can't you tell that atop the HIGHEST mountain
or at the bottom of the DEEPEST ocean..
I'd SWIM that deep or CLIMB that high
just to PROVE my love is potent...
Fantastic FOCUS finally honed in
on the woman who OWNS my every moment...
Inside my SOUL she lives and breathes as
TANDEM heartbeats become our main component...
In an EVERLASTING love
not even De'Lure could dream up or imagine...
Delicate decisive deals
are duly DRENCHED in unforgettable passion...
Marriage is NOT our end game
but the beginning of our FORTUNE...
To be rich in LOVE is to be rich for LIFE
no man can have MY PORTION...
She's mine and yes Lord she's FINE
but I could find that woman's BEAUTY
even if I was BLIND
a love so DIVINE
I don't even need the services of mine eyes
to dive DEEP within her soul to find
every single thing my God designed
for me, her, for us if you feel a little jealous now
you should it'll only get worse
I LOVED that woman from hello
and will from inside the hearse

Be it mine
or my Valentine's final day above ground
Her voice and heart's beat
will die my FAVORITE sounds
My funny, funny Valentine
they don't sell in stores what you're WORTH to me
To do you JUSTICE I'd have to buy you
entire OCEANS, MOUNTAINS, and SEAS
Live inside my love for you
it's all yours for the taking
And this my LOVE is your Valentine's Day poem
SORRY to have kept you waiting

I love you ETERNALLY

"Eyes and Minds"

(4-13-16)

Mental Apex

All the eyes on you

constantly stabbing you like darts...

The FALSIFIED verbal care packages

they DELIVER as if they had hearts...

Don't let em' start...

They speak on your PAST

when your PRESENT and FUTURE is too bright

for them to withstand...

In their hearts, they KNOW

*they'd rather ride your coattails away from a life
so BLAND...*

Grandstand... You can't SAVE them all

but you can TEACH anyone to dream...

Your TESTIMONY a fiery display

that ANY soul can be redeemed...

Bursting at the seams...

No one understands the TIP of the pyramid

until the clouds OPEN and they mentally ascend...

Showing face and then hiding tail from the angels

De'Lure

is NEVER something I recommend...

This is not a trend...

The laws and ideologies I DEFEND

are happy, healthy, and efficient living...

Break your own heart first

then REBUILD you to find everything that was missing...

Thoughtful wishing...

Your life is a MISSION

are you failing or passing...

Crashing can be a good thing

as long as there's progressive WISDOM you're amassing...

Your life is flashing...

Relationship goals due to

mental, parental, and emotional HOLES...

Daughters with NO dads and sons

who've become their mother's DAMAGED loopholes...

Loose souls...

Little girls

who NEVER knew daddy's love at all...

Little boys

EXPECTED to catch their lonely mother's whenever they fall...

Unacceptable... Blurred responsibilities

due to MISSING paternal figures in the home...

Loves and disciplines that throughout MATURATION

remain unknown...

All silently condoned...

If you gave BIRTH to a kid

to TRY to keep a man...

Do not then DESTROY the child

because the FATHER had other plans...

I mean DAMN...

What De'Lure should do

is keep PAVING a new way...

I can't preach and teach YET

or adequately manufacture a new day...

Child's play...

Stupid is STILL the new cool

De'Lure

this fact remains the same...

Hiding things from them in BOOKS has become routine

and the cycle DESTRUCTIVELY mundane...

But the BLAME game...

Each man and woman

has to CHOOSE to be awakened...

If you're awaiting or expecting

a spontaneous PUSH you're sadly mistaken...

Poetic painstaking...

Break away from

your past, present, and pain causing PEERS...

No validation from them is REQUIRED

your life matters GROW tired of the tears...

And all your very REAL fears...

Live and Love

SINCERE

"Black Tears"

(4-25-17)

Every tear you ever cried

eventually dried up and died

I empathize but also realize real lies

Reveal real lives as lights shine

To unveil foreign shadows and signs

Keep in mind you only get one mind

So, trying to find divine in swine

Is a crime against your own mind in its own right

Love is a fight

But try to choose your battles wisely

If you realize your heart is on the wrong beat

Change the tune but leave quietly

You could waste a lifetime

Bleeding for the wrong person's affection

When all the while your true soulmate

Was waiting in the opposite direction

If you could I would tell you to

Gather up all your black tears and painful lessons

And carry them atop your head

Until the moment, you can shower them

On the head of your true love as unconditional blessings...

DESTINY

"*Perception*"

(12-19-16)

De'Lure

Perception is reality

so TRUTH is whatever PEOPLE believe...

And in turn you and I can ONLY aspire to be

what ANOTHER BEING conceives...

Bitch please...

This is TREASON

especially when this is MY SEASON...

I NEVER stress over the egregious, facetious, CREATURES

that try to DEMEAN me...

Nahh I shed a few tears honestly

*but it all adds to the FABRIC that is creating the
SUPREME me...*

Cut from a different texture and cloth

I ALWAYS rise again...

I buck EVERY trend, subconsciously in their minds

I IMPLANT eternal AMENDS...

My FUTURE will debilitate

all who wish me to FAIL...

Watching me was NEVER a good look

we never belonged on the SAME SCALE...

All I had to do was be ME

and SUCCESS has FOUND me...

My art, faith, and love

are ABOUNDING...

Whilst my DEMONS are DROWNING

in their own BLOOD and HATRED...

Sooner THAN later they gotta FACE IT

I am the MATRIX...

See, living FAITHLESS and SHAPELESS

is beyond BASIC...

This level of SATISFACTION

is utterly AMAZING...

In his or her mind at any given time.

"Fruitful Waters"

(5-11-16)

As the fruitful waters

sprinkle forth from your fingertips...

Pay no mind to those

who refuse to gather it up or sip...

Just continue to drip

without even parting your lips...

Those in tune with life

will never forget...

Pyramids are more than world wonders

as is the human mind...

From its peak, you can seek

the things you never thought you'd find...

Over 2.3 million stones come together

to solidify beauty and greatness...

The blood and whispers trapped inside them

can never be faded...

The Eye is open and always has been...

We all make the mistake

of mistaking our own most cardinal sin...

Walk with me across the endless black sand

the waters no longer need us...

We give birth to the wind from our lungs

De'Lure

as does a mother's womb to a fetus...

No longer run away from the wisdom and truth

the Enlightened Ones try to teach you...

As They soar Their wings only spread

in hopes to finally reach you...

Nothing you've ever known

is the way to the TRUTH...

Your most private thoughts

are obvious and so uncouth...

If the Darkness is in you at birth

you can run forever if you like...

But it never leaves your soul

no matter how long and hard you fight...

Our Words are not Our own

they're chosen for Us...

Always have been that's why

they're as pure as the clouds We often touch...

A baby is born

with the wisdom of the Eye...

Before he first speaks

that knowledge will always die...

We can remember it all now

if we open our minds and our hearts...

Destruction or Dominance

is a choice we make from the start

"*Josiah*"

(7-17-16)

Someone please tell him
he's my pride and joy...
He'll never remember
all the candy and toys...
My hugs and my words
are all so real...
Let those be amongst the memories
he'll always recollect and feel...
One Christmas two Christmas
daddy will always be there...
I would run, fly, or swim
to hold you by your granny's chimney with care...
On Christmas Eve rocking you
until you slumber in my arms...
I'd die and lay down my legacy
before I'd ever let you know harm...
My passion for your life drives me
and has made me a better man...
Become a billionaire in twenty years
I'll never know a better plan...
When I look at you
I see myself as a child...
Charismatic, full of energy,
with a huge heart so wild...
You are the new me
the possibilities for you are endless...
They'll never be ready for you;
son you'll render this world defenseless...
I'm instilling everything I am in you;
son I swear you are my all...
Don't you ever be afraid to jump at life
daddy will catch you if you fall...
When I'm not there I hope someone tells you
daddy writes books he's out chasing his dreams...
But in my dreams, I'm in your room

De'Lure

> *watching you sleep peacefully as I sing...*
> *Sweet De'Lure nursery rhymes*
> *from a book, I haven't written yet...*
> *As your mother hums, along with me*
> *the three of us a connected set...*
> *One day you'll be so great*
> *and I promise son you'll go far...*
> *And the reason daddy knows you'll be great...*
> *Is because you already are..."*

I love you Josiah Aiden

"First Things First"

(5-16-2015)

De'Lure

I WAS YOUR FIRST

THAT FACT REMAINS THE SAME

AND I DON'T EVEN KNOW HOW WE BROKE UP

THAT SEEMS STRANGE

AND FLOWERS FELL FROM THE CAR CEILING

WHEN I DEFLOWERED YOU

I FELT LIKE I EMPOWERED YOU

TO TOWER OVER THE COWARDLY DUDES

WHO TRIED TO DEVALUE YOU

SEE GIRL I TREASURE YOU

FAR BEYOND ANY MENTAL ESCAPADE

TO WANNA PLEASURE YOU

I WANT TO EMOTIONALLY MEASURE YOU

WHEN I LOOK INTO YOUR EYES

AND FIND YOUR SOUL

I FIND MY HEAVEN'S DEW

YOU'RE EVERY BIT AS HEAVENLY

AS EVERY ANGEL IN THE SKY

AND EVERY MAN ON EARTH'S FANTASY

FROM YOUR HIPS, TO YOUR LIPS, TO YOUR EYES

BUT YOUR MIND FLIES

FAR BEYOND ALL THE BEAUTIFUL BLUE BUTTERFLIES

MY EYES SPY IN DISTANT SUMMER SET SKIES

SENTIMENTAL SOMMERSAULTS

MY HEART FLIPS

EVERYTIME IT DIPS INTO THE POOLS OF YOUR EYES

IT SKIPS

THEN MY HEART DRIPS

HONEY DOWN THE SMALL OF YA BACK

AND IN BETWEEN YA LIPS

JUST A FANTASY NOW

OUR LOVE HAS LONG PAST AWAY

BUT FACTS REMAIN FACTS

I'LL BE YOUR FIRST TILL MY DYING DAY

"*Systematic*"

(2-7-17)

Alone fades into Lonely, fades into lost, fades into depression...

Regression is pressing onward

like a small funeral procession...

Don't miss the message or the lesson...

The people who claim they love you

are exempt from discretion...

Blessings in disguise

you don't have to try to become wise...

The eyes and lies of your tribe

will guide your lives...

Likewise, your vibes transcribe

your demise or your rise...

Butterflies and buttermilk pies just permeate and justify

the emotional crimes from which we hide...

Our focus remains on the irrelevant

rather than becoming prevalent...

Sometimes a settlement

is just a mask for devilment...

Systematic betterment would be heaven sent

a metaphoric Band-Aid

for all the self-inflicted detriment...

Watch How Far...

(Halloween 2016)

Throwing LYRICAL steel darts

at THE EMPTY SPACES that

were meant for your hearts...

That's just the start of the art

I'm about to cart off on you Tards...

No car, no bar, no star

is too far out of my reach so don't start...

Fall apart with DEMON HEARTS

I'll never be a man apart...

My art is the launching pad and the connecting strand

to EVERYTHING I am...

No matter what the devil's try

I FLY because I can...

Panoramic views from my peripheral

leaves no snake invisible...

You can only take joy in another man's PAIN

if you yourself are miserable AND INSANE...

At the end of the day

YOUR LIFE is still YOUR LIFE...

Your hate is IRRELEVANT

but does it really help you sleep at night...

He won't ever give me

De'Lure

more than I can bear...

My STRENGTH and WILL

Have ALWAYS been tested I swear...

NOT that you'd CARE

if in fact you were aware...

Of all the FACTS and all the STACKS

you still wouldn't treat me FAIR...

But who cares

I haven't NEEDED to work for another soul in YEARS...

I live and breathe MY DREAMS

all the things your mediocre ass FEARS...

You call those careers

and I'm not even the type

to knock the next mfs life...

But INVISIBLE GHOSTS

wanna talk about my conquerable STRIFE...

No, I stride with pride

that asshole MENTALITY is why I ALWAYS RISE...

God, it feels so good to YOU devils

to attempt to TEAR someone down ABOVE YOU...

But you and I know the TRUTH

YOUR MISERY stems from the living FACT

that nobody EVER loved you...

You were born unlovable

only here to SEEK, KILL, and DESTROY...

How can you actively take down a genius

who no one can employ...

Sign my own checks

I was put here to be in charge...

My future BRIGHTER than eternal illumination

INJECTED with a hundred million STARS...

Watch! How! Far!!!

"BREAK OUT!!!"

(4-28-17)

You never wanna be the one

somebody else has to DUMB something down for...

With all the academic RICHES this planet is ENRICHED with

why are so many of us still mentally POOR...

I know you heard my metaphor

about how I used to feel like an EYE SORE...

And now I SOAR through every open door...

Elevating to every floor

this INSTINCT was IN me when I was BORN...

I just had to UNLOCK it

WATCH it EVOLVE and now NO ONE can stop it...

I don't mind all the gawkin' or being a hot topic...

I've single handily ENGINEERED an earning potential

that's gonna land me PERMANENTLY in the tropics...

But I'm not on this JOURNEY to be alone

I want a whole ARMY of AFFLUENT dreamers...

I'm not one of the CRABS in the barrel I hope everybody

at some point owns a Lambo or at least a Beamer...

Why go through life ANGRY because others

SEEM to make HAPPINESS look so easy...

I never had RESPECT for a hateful flunky

I'd rather another man RISE UP and beat me...

Do what I do BETTER than me

if you LOVE what I love TOO...

But if you're only capable of JEALOUS SPITE

don't WORRY about

how GOOD my feet feel in MY SHOES...

You just stay LOCAL

and continue to DETERIORATE the way dudes like you do...

And maybe one day you'll OUT GROW

that crab barrel and INFUSE a new you...

That's what Kings are supposed to do...

I'ma just keep building these INVISIBLE PYRAMIDS and stay TRUE...

You Be YOU

"*Inescapable*"

(7-17-16)

De'Lure

Lady never question me

on matters of the heart...

I was born with the aptitude

to tear this world apart...

Winding roads in my mind

leading to places you could never go...

Born embedded with wise rhythmic concepts

you could never ever know...

Godly flow

I wonder if they'll ever know before I go...

Or will my name get the same treatment

as Picasso and Van Gogh...

How come we almost never love genius

while it remains live and tangible...

Actively express satisfaction and awe

as the fruits of my spirit escape from my mandible...

Creating whole worlds in my mind

is a mild day, I just call it art...

When they get lost in the depth and texture of my words,

I call that my heart...

Reading becomes a lifestyle

when the words are from the soul of an artist...

The first word I write in a novel

To me is always the hardest...

Then it all flows like golden waterfalls

the passion never ends...

Then I fall so deep inside the flow of me

that NOT writing becomes a sin...

They all claim to have beautiful minds

but only the children of the light can TRULY attain such...

Blinded by egos and alternate realities

they seem to me out of touch...

Oh, but she, the one with the potential

to make his life and world complete...

The one who wants the spotlight

even when he would rather be discreet...

HER HEART embraces a precious secret

and the sole key to my soul...

In the fibers of her eyes I there find

the essence of my God given goals...

Run away young woman

deep inside my open mind...

And in return I'll gift you eternally

with the purest love, you could ever find...

"*Freed*"

(3-11-2017)

Understand your own wisdom

and enjoy your individualism...

You can't speak into existence

what others are clearly missing...

You were chosen and gifted

to see the lighted path...

Financials elevating daily

just do the math...

Human calculator with a clear vision

of what your future holds...

Without selling your soul

live bold as your dreams unfold...

Stick to the blueprint is the war cry...

In a couple of years even your most sincere haters

will rectify and testify...

You're a better guy

than their eyes wanted to see...

It's hard embodying

everything they wanted to be...

They damn sure didn't want this for me...

But multi-dimensional imagination

is my pedigree...

De'Lure

Don't need female dogs petting me

I see my Queen...

Loving the wrong woman isn't the root of evil

but the very seed...

I live to make your senses bleed

my illumination freed indeed...

Found my hunger first in my childish greed

now it's my soul I please...

I was created to build up a people

but Jesus saves and I don't...

You can't inject true prosperity

into a world full of clones...

Mind blown, everything I own

was built upon shattered bones...

I no longer shed tears

Pleasantly alone is my comfort zone...

My tribe will reunite

after I finish planting the seventh seed...

Twelve books in six years

my dream is me...

Not arrogance just evolution

of self-collusion and inclusion...

After years of abuse and mental pollution

the truth is I'm never losing...

Again

"Open the Sky"

(11-20-16)

WE CLOSE OUR EYES TO OPEN UP OUR MINDS

AS THE SKY CRACKS OPEN...

IT SEEMS THEN TO SOME

THAT ALL OF OUR DREAMS ARE BROKEN...

BUT CONTRARY TO POPULAR BELIEF

THIS IS EXACTLY WHAT WE WERE HOPIN'...

I'M NEVER LOSIN FOCUS

UNTIL THE WHOLE TEAM'S BELLIES AND POCKETS
ARE SWOLLEN...

THIS RIGHT HERE

IS MORE THAN JUST AN OMEN...

I NEED YOU TO HONE IN

WE'RE ALL GROWN MEN...

AND LADIES SO LET THIS SOAK IN

UNTIL WE'RE ALL GLOWIN'...

AND NAHH I AIN' GROANIN'

I'M JUST EPISODIN'...

GIVIN YOU A PIECE OF MY MIND

ITS UP TO YOU TO DECODE IT...

MY MIND IS TRANSCENDENT AND INNOVATIVE

MY CREATIVITY OVERFLOWING...

SO JUST LIKE COACH PJ FLEK 2016

I JUST KEEP ON ROWING...

WESTERN MICHIGAN IF YOU NASTY

I GROW HIGHER EVERYDAY...

WE ALL ONLY GET ONE OAR

*SUCCESS IS DIRECTLY CORRELATED TO PADDLING
THE SAME WAY...*

MY BOAT IS YOUR BOAT

THERE ARE BIBLICAL MUSINGS

IN EVERY POEM, I SLAY...

SOMETIMES I DREAM OF GENIES IN A DIFFERENT WORLD

HOW COME WE GOTTA WATCH RERUNS

JUST TO FIND OUR HAPPY DAYS...

THERE ARE OVER A MILLION WAYS TO BECOME SUCCESSFUL

WHOMEVER BLEEDS THE MOST

RECEIVES THE BIGGEST REWARD...

I COULD HAVE ON WINGTIPS

OR A PAIR OF JORDAN CONCORDS

AND EITHER WAY I'D SLICE YOU UP

WITH THIS DOUBLE-EDGED SWORD...

AND I'M NEVER TONGUE IN CHEEK

MY INTENT IS TO LEAVE

LASTING MENTAL ABRASIONS AND SORES...

WHICH HURTS MORE DYING MISERABLE

OR LIVING INSIDE OF A HOLY WAR...

MOST INTELLECTUALS WOULD HAVE YOU BELIEVE

CHRIST IS JUST A MYTH...

I KNOW HE EXISTS BECAUSE HE SPEAKS TO ME

AND HAS GIVEN ME ETERNAL GIFTS...

THAT LIFT, DRIFT, AND SIFT ME

THROUGH ALL THE WORLD'S BULLSHIT

"Malnourished"

(11-11-16)

Once we fall away into the DARKNESS

their SCREAMS no longer sound as sweet...

When LOVE becomes HATE

you ACCEPT your trying troubles as a TREAT...

No one DESERVES that much RAIN

he should have DROWNED long ago...

No one gives a damn at all

the BLESSED row along in their sturdy boats...

They said he's a MONSTER

so it MUST be so...

When some look in HIS FACE

it doesn't quite show...

Give it a while

maybe the CRAZY comes on slow...

Don't lend him a HEART

you'll DISRUPT his DESTRUCTIVE flow...

Gather up his ART

set it all ABLAZE...

The good all die young

his mind a BASTARDLY maze...

De'Lure

Close your eyes and LISTEN to his WORDS

of poetic INJUSTICE...

Unapologetically imperfect

a once BEAUTIFUL MIND now hideously corrupted...

MENTALLY Malnourished*!!*

"*Purple Nightmares*"

(8-24-15)

Purple Nightmares of a Visionary

Real devils

trapped inside the skies of their own minds...

Stagnant lies

dipped in milk and honey lullabies...

I cry for the future of man

no longer strong enough to fly...

Weed smoke and ignorant music

progressively molding a generation of flies...

Flies will do anything

eat shit and go beyond...

People are no longer people

no one feels the need to bond...

A man choosing to educate himself

no longer a pro, but THE ULTIMATE con...

So, do minds like mine remain trapped

in poems like this and just move on...

Sensitivity has been deemed unacceptable...

The heart of man

has been rendered undetectable...

Guns, drugs, and violence

are viewed as sexy and cool...

While the masses sit back idly

watching our world destroyed by fools...

Rise up,

awaken from the ease of a life of mediocrity...

Never claim you want more

when you romanticize a life of poverty...

Even if you give a weak-minded man

endless money he'll find a way to lose it all...

Sit him high up in the clouds with real angels,

give him wings he'll still fall...

Exercise your brain my friend,

you're not a savage or an inanimate doll...

AND Exorcise your demons

before they grow, feed, and evolve... #Resolve

De'Lure

"TMBA Dreams Realized"

(11-9-16)

Mental Apex

My eyes cried 100,000 times

the first time I saw Take My Breath Away live...

Although closed were my eyes

it didn't deflate my triumphant glide...

Pride aside my heart opened wide and smiled...

I never tried to deny my shine

as I was peacefully beguiled....

No words can describe

how my emotions dive on the rollercoaster that is my mind...

From the front row, I was finally awakened

but even before I was never blind...

Trying times had to find, confine, and then define my life

before I could become king...

A cracked crown is still a crown

and a true champion always gets a ring...

My show was magnificent

everyone in attendance had a glorious time...

Even the demons scattered about

were moved beyond their silent defiant eyes...

Creative genius pleasantly painted itself across an open stage

before my watery gaze...

For two full hours, my dreams met fruition

with my beloved characters on full display...

The actors owned their lines and roles

I believed they were my creations...

I knew one day the world would know my name

as I drowned in painful patience...

Happiness and success will always run adjacent

while blind hate and contentment

have zero correlation...

Be a changing agent and appreciate the speed of love

in which our hearts are capable of racing...

And then, allow me to take your breath away...

"Cold Place"

(10-30-16)

The world

is such a COLD and CRUEL place...

Pain and FEAR

have become commonplace...

Depression

is a common face...

Disappointment and glorified cyber bullying

the only mainstays...

Can anyone

eternally take the pain away...

Erase the rain away...

Make their mouths hush

until they know what to say...

Lies don't care who tell them

never have never will...

Run away into your own grave

and forever be still...

See cause then you can't hear the noise

they're so happy to hear dumb sh#t...

But these are the realities

of what 2016-17 comes with...

Jesus come quick

let the old-world die...

Then all the ones who judge us all

will fall to their knees and cry...

God is all I ever needed

because of Him I can AND DO shut the devil out...

The numbness to blind hatred

leads to a lasting emotional drought...

Suicide would ice the cake

and further the lying lynch mob's cause...

Instead take your mind away

and bleed deep into the stars...

Understand that killing you

is medicine to some...

They hate to see anyone prosper

And they often end dreams with guns...

Or twisted blown up lies

"Target Practice"

(4-3-16)

Mental Apex

They seldom understand

the minds of the truly gifted...

Nor do they comprehend all the struggles

through which we've sifted...

Genius is a mind state

it's definitely addictive in nature...

My thoughts can move mountains

and construct unfathomable sky scrapers...

I'll be a billionaire

before I ever live half a century...

I cannot fail

I'm allergic to the concept mentally...

Have you ever gone to sleep

only to see your whole future in shades of gold...

Have you ever felt certain

that you came from a supreme and broken mold...

Once you tap into and crack open your skull

you have to give them the yolk...

Teach them and raise them up

so, they will no longer think and live like common folk...

A lady once told me dreams are never realistic

you have to be one in a million...

De'Lure

I smiled politely and told her baby I'm that one

and my words and dreams are worth billions...

You can be anything you want

I pray you don't choose to just get by...

I will stop at nothing to live peacefully

way up in the sky...

My own Heaven on Earth

before it's my time to die...

Until that beautiful second

with my own wings, I'll glide and guide...

If you hear me

it's because you're supposed to...

If you can't

I blame what you've been exposed to...

They say our nation is dumbed down

but are you one of the ones they're referring to...

When they say, this is generation X

are you deserving of that title too...

We can control popular public perception

by being more positive every day...

Just as I'll mold and control my legacy

with every word, I'll ever say...

About the Author

De'Lure is a dreamer who writes with his heart and a very realistic imagination. His first passion was acting, but from that love spawned an even deeper passion for the art of writing. The imagery he uses to create stories is packed with all the components of legendary writing careers. Expect great things from De'Lure.

De'Lure

If you enjoyed this novel you should check out these other AMAZING titles by De'Lure

Onyx Cielo: Book 1 -The Tree of Transformation- (Fantasy)
Take My Breath Away: Orlando Nights –RELOADED- (Realistic Romance/ Drama/ Erotica)
Take My Breath Away 2: When Love Calls (Realistic Romance/ Drama/ Erotica)
Take My Breath Away 3: Save me from My Past (Realistic Romance/ Drama/ Erotica)
Passion Absolute –Radicon's Princess- (Realistic Romance/ Drama/Erotica)
De'Lure Shorts & Poem (Poetry/Drama/Short Stories)
De'Lure Shorts & Poems 2 (Poetry/Drama/Short Stories)
He Without Sin(Romance/Mystery/Suspense)
Mental Apex -Invisible Pyramids- (Poetic Perfection)
Kissed (Realistic/ Drama/ Murder/ Mystery)

Available through Amazon.com, Barnes&noble.com, and many other retailers. Signed copies can also be ordered directly from the author.
Email: ceom.love@gmail.com
FB: Published De'Lure

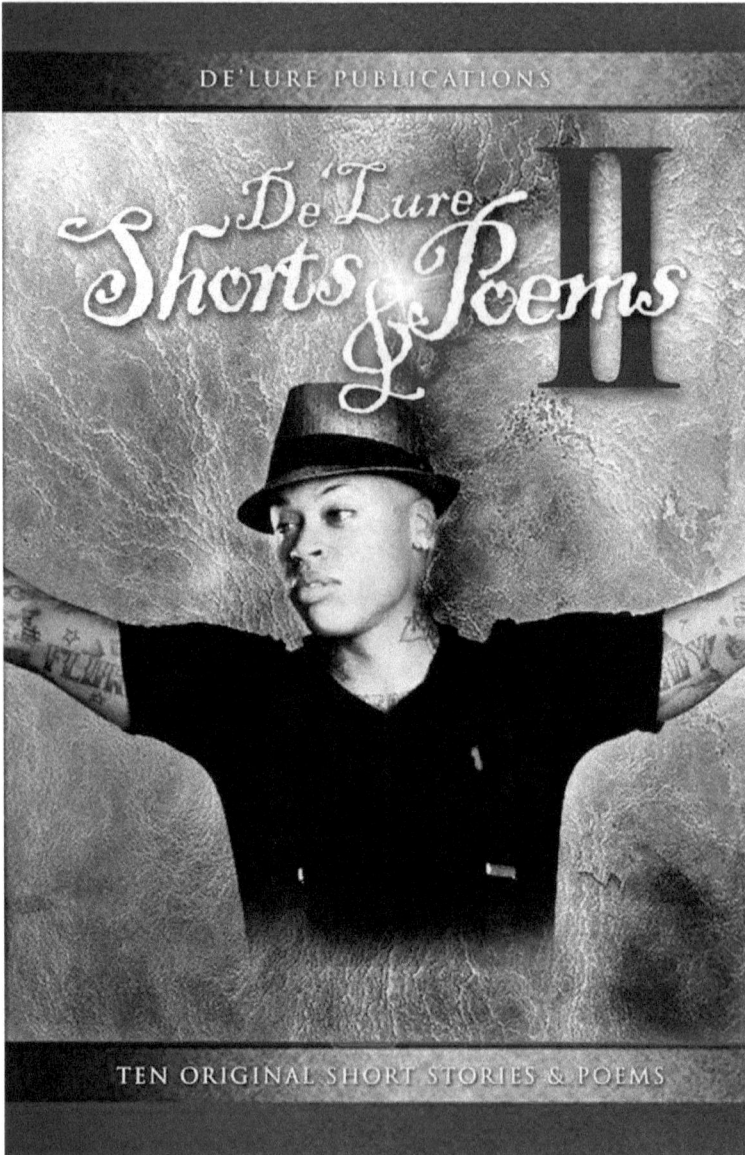